627 Challenging Sports Trivia Questions

Seven Phoenix, Ph.D., Editor

DEDICATION

This book is dedicated to all the sports trivia junkies out there.

Table of Contents

PREFACE

This volume of trivia came about for people who are seeking no-nonsense trivia questions for their own pub trivia night, personal entertainment, or to play with family and friends. These questions are essentially a "B-Side" to my main volumes of trivia, *American Pub Trivia*, of which two highly engaging and entertaining volumes have been published.

627 Challenging Sports Trivia Questions

Questions 1-10

1. What pitcher threw a perfect game for the New York Yankees in the 1956 World Series?

2. Who beat Cal 2-1 in the first women's college basketball game in 1896?

3. Who future hockey legend signed with the Indianapolis Racers in 1978 at age 17 because he was too young for the NHL?

4. He's best known as coach of the Miami Dolphins, a team he led to two Super Bowl Championships, including the incredible 1972 perfect season.

5. Who was the third person in the broadcast booth with Howard Cosell and Don Meredith when "Monday Night Football" debuted in 1970?

6. Who did Spud Webb play for when he led the NBA in free-throw shooting in 1995?

7. On December 25, 1972, this team defeated the Kansas City Chiefs in one of the longest games in NFL history by kicking a field goal to end the game after 82 minutes, 40 seconds of playing time.

8. What football term is often used to describe the USC sweep play in the mid to late 1960s, but was actually created to describe Missouri's wide sweep?

9. What does the "A" in the Oakland A's MLB team name stands for?

10. Now that Orlando is home to the Wizarding World of Harry Potter at Universal Studios Orlando the name for this Orlando-based NBA team makes more sense.

Answers 1-10

1. Don Larsen

2. Stanford

3. Wayne Gretzky

4. Don Shula

5. Keith Jackson

6. Kings

7. Miami Dolphins

8. Student Body Right

9. Athletics

10. Magic

Questions 11-20

11. The North American Soccer League (NASL) existed from 1968-1984. The team from Vancouver was called?

12. The Lumberjack World Championships have been held annually since 1960 in Hayward in which U.S. state?

13. Who was the first NBA player to win three MVPs in a row?

14. What country hosts the Hopman Cup Tournament?

15. What coach's team, D.C. United, dominated the early years of the MLS, winning the Cup Championship three of the first four years?

16. Who had the longest interception return for a touchdown in Super Bowl history with a 100-yard sramble against Arizona in Super Bowl XLIII?

17. CD Chivas USA plays Major League Soccer in what U.S. state?

18. It's awarded to each season's winner of the college football game between the Colorado State University Rams and the University of Wyoming Cowboys.

19. Who had his number (22) officially retired by the Harlem Globetrotters in February 2008?

20. In Super Bowl XLII with less than 2 minutes remaining against the undefeated Patriots, what WR made a legal catch that has since been named "The Helmet Catch?"

Answers 11-20

11. Whitecaps

12. Wisconsin

13. Bill Russell

14. Australia

15. Bruce Arena

16. James Harrison

17. California

18. Bronze Boot

19. Curly Neal

20. David Tyree

Questions 21-30

21. Major League Soccer's Designated Player Rule was created for the 2007 season, when what ballyhooed English star joined the L.A. Galaxy?

22. Who threw down a one-handed dunk against the Florida Gators in 2012 to become just the second woman to dunk in an NCAA Women's Basketball Tournament?

23. Who won back-to-back MVP awards for the 2008-2009 and 2009-2010 NBA seasons?

24. How many seconds do you have to inbounds the ball in basketball?

25. Because LiveStrong Sporting Park was not ready for the 2011 MLS season, what team played their first 10 games on the road, losing all but one?

26. What nickname was given to the New York Yankees' greats Ruth, Gehrig, DiMaggio and Mantle?

27. In 1962, this famous golfer became the first man to win an LPGA event when he defeated Mickey Wright by five strokes at the par-3 Royal Poinciana Invitational.

28. What team did Mike Mercer play for when he kicked the first field goal in Super Bowl history?

29. This NHL team is also known as Le Bleu-Blanc-Rouge, Le CH, Les Glorieux, Le Grand Club, Les Habitants, La Sainte-Flanelle and Le Tricolore.

30. This golfer broke 80 at age 8, 70 at age 11, and then won the Junior World Championships six times before turning pro in August of 1996.

Answers 21-30

21. David Beckham

22. Brittney Griner

23. Lebron James

24. 5

25. Sporting KC

26. Sultans of Swat

27. Sam Snead

28. Kansas City Chiefs

29. Canadiens

30. Tiger Woods

Questions 31-40

31. What Hall of Fame-bound QB was reluctantly released by the Indianapolis Colts in 2012, after he missed the entire 2011 season recovering from neck surgery?

32. What NBA team did Ray Allen play for when he nailed 269 three-point shots during the 2005-2006 season?

33. Because of their black logo, this Atlanta NFL team is often referred to as the "Dirty Birds."

34. As a popular locale for Scandinavian American culture, this NFL team in Minnesota would likely have been Leif Ericsson's favorite.

35. What 2 quarterbacks broke Dan Marino's 1984 single season passing yards record of 5,084 yards in 2011?

36. Who was drafted first in the 2010 NFL Draft at the quarterback position?

37. How many seasons did Michael Jordan play for the Washington Wizards?

38. He played from 1954-1974 for the Milwaukee and Atlanta Braves, and then the Milwaukee Brewers in 1976. Name this player who finished his career with 755 career homeruns.

39. A name-the-team contest resulted in this NFL team name, a reference to the pirate legends of Southwest Florida. They didn't win their first game until the thirteenth week of their second season, starting 0-26.

40. What professional sport was first televised on W2XBS to approximately 500 TV owners in New York City on October 22, 1939?

Answers 31-40

31. Peyton Manning

32. Seattle Supersonics

33. Falcons

34. Vikings

35. Brees & Brady

36. Sam Bradford

37. 2

38. Hank Aaron

39. Buccaneers

40. Football

Questions 41-50

41. This famous Arkansan was a professional baseball player who once won 30 games in one season (1934). He played for the Cardinals, Cubs and Browns.

42. As the Motor City, it's only fitting that Detroit would name its NBA team after this motor part.

43. What score did Tiger Woods post on the very first hole of the 1997 Masters Tournament?

44. Once a New York team, named to rhyme with the MLB's Mets and NFL's Jets, this NBA team relocated to Brooklyn in 2012.

45. Who is the only hockey player to score 200 points in a season... four times?

46. The 1947 World Series was the first to be televised. Though it was only broadcast in a few markets, it's estimated that nearly 4 million people watched what team beat the Brooklyn Dodgers in seven games?

47. What group was the first to cross the English Channel in an inflatible kangaroo?

48. This NBA player is one of the best point guards of all time. He set record for most career assists and steals during his 19-year career with the Utah Jazz.

49. James Naismith is most commonly credited with inventing which sport?

50. Sometimes called "The Amazin's" by their fans, what National League MLB team makes their home in New York?

Answers 41-50

41. Dizzy Dean

42. Pistons

43. Bogey

44. Nets

45. Wayne Gretzky

46. New York Yankees

47. Dangerous Sports Club

48. John Stockton

49. Basketball

50. Mets

Questions 51-60

51. What category of drugs has come to be publicly associated with the likes of Jose Canseco, Gary Sheffield, Mark McGwire, Barry Bonds, Jason Giambi and Rafael Palmeiro?

52. In 2011, President Obama invited this Super Bowl XX winning team from the 1985 season to the White House since it hadn't made the visit in 1986 due to the timing of the Space Shuttle Challenger disaster.

53. Who was the first Puerto Rican born golfer to be inducted into the World Golf Hall of Fame?

54. In the 2000 MLS season, what goalkeeper recorded the longest shutout streak in MLS history by keeping the ball out of the net for 681 minutes?

55. Who was commissioned as the official Olympic artist by the U.S. team in 2006?

56. At 1996 Summer Olympics in Atlanta, he won the men's tennis gold medal, making him the first man to win the Golden Slam (winning all four Grand Slam events and an Olympic gold medal).

57. Who drafted Eli Manning with the first pick in the 2004 NFL Draft?

58. Out of respect for this former Baltimore Colts QB only one Baltimore Ravens player (Scott Mitchell) has worn his number, 19.

59. What was the name of the schooner that won the America's Cup for the New York Yacht Club the very first time? It happened in 1851.

60. What is this signature song of the Harlem Globetrotters?

Answers 51-60

51. Steroids

52. Chicago Bears

53. Chi Chi RodrÃ-guez

54. Tony Meola

55. Alfred Gockel

56. Andre Agassi

57. San Diego Chargers

58. Johnny Unitas

59. America

60. Sweet Georgia Brown

Questions 61-70

61. What team did the United States defeat to win its very first hockey gold medal at the Winter Olympics?

62. What baseball pitcher leads the MLB for most all time losses ?

63. Who is the only golfer to win the U.S. Open in 3 different decades?

64. What basketball shot was made illegal in college games in 1967?

65. The first fight televised on "HBO Boxing After Dark" was in 1973 when George Foreman took the heavyweight title by knocking out this boxer in the second round.

66. What winter sport combines cross-country skiing with rifle shooting?

67. Who was the Indy Racing League's "Rookie of the Year" in 2005?

68. Colorado's soccer team is one of the ten charter clubs of Major League Soccer. They surged to the MLS Cup title in 2010, riding out the rough waters of competition, which they should be used to given this team name.

69. Whose last match was a lost to Benjamin Becker in the 2006 U.S. Open?

70. This 5-time NBA championship winner was just as well known for his rainbow-colored hair and tattoos as he was for his rebounding skills.

Answers 61-70

61. Czechoslovakia

62. Cy Young

63. Jack Nicklaus

64. Slam Dunk

65. Joe Frazier

66. Biathlon

67. Danica Patrick

68. Rapids

69. Andre Agassi

70. Dennis Rodman

Questions 71-80

71. What city hosted the Super Bowl three times out of the first five?

72. He was traded from the Blue Jays to the Phillies before the 2010 season. Name this ace nicknamed "Doc" who pitched the 20th perfect game in MLB history on May 29th, 2010.

73. Whose home run record did Mark McGwire beat in 1998 with 70 home runs?

74. What hockey player wore number 99 from 1979-1988 with the Edmonton Oilers?

75. How many Hall of Famers did Carl Hubbell strike out in succession in the 1934 All-Star Game?

76. What's the only major championship Lee Trevino failed to win?

77. In the 1950s, the 49ers backfield consisted of 4 future Hall of Fame members: Y.A. Tittle, John Henry Johnson, Hugh McElhenny & Joe Perry. What monetary nickname did this group have?

78. The team was founded in 2000, becoming the first NHL franchise in Minnesota since the North Stars moved to Dallas in 1993.

79. Who did the Denver Broncos beat in 1997 to win their first Super Bowl?

80. Who was the winning American League pitcher in the 2008 MLB All-Star Game that went 15 innings? He also played in the World Series that year.

Answers 71-80

71. Miami

72. Roy Halladay

73. Roger Maris

74. Wayne Gretzky

75. 5

76. The Masters

77. Million Dollar Backfield

78. Wild

79. Green Bay Packers

80. Scott Kazmir

Questions 81-90

81. How many MVP awards did Michael Jordan win in his career?

82. What proud network was the first to broadcast the World Series in color?

83. Watching some of the same players compete on the court who also competed on the gridiron, this originator of basketball said, "Oh, my gracious! They are murdering my game!"

84. What was commonly referred to as "Chinese Boxing" before the 1960s?

85. University of Missouri basketball coach Norm Stewart would traditionally have his players stay in Missouri before playing at what school, so as not to contribute money to the state's economy?

86. How much money did the champion receive for winning the first Masters Tournament?

87. What NFL player returned four kicks for touchdowns in four consecutive games?

88. This Major League Baseball player was nicknamed "The Chicken Man."

89. In what sport do the players vote for the recipient of the Lester Pearson award?

90. Who was the first Minnesota Twin to win the Cy Young Award?

Answers 81-90

81. 5

82. NBC

83. James Naismith

84. Kung Fu

85. Kansas

86. 1500

87. Dante Hall

88. Wade Boggs

89. NHL

90. Jim Perry

Questions 91-100

91. This NBA team was formed in 1988 as an expansion franchise, along with the Orlando Magic, as one of two teams simultaneously created in the state of Florida.

92. Who was on the cover of the Madden NFL 1998 game?

93. What card is Alexander the Great supposedly represented by in a deck of cards?

94. This famous Arkansan is a retired professional basketball player, considered one of the best small forwards of all time, who was instrumental in 6 NBA titles for the Bulls.

95. Who is the only player to have his number retired across the entire NHL?

96. This British athlete won the silver medal in the 1500m dash at 1920 Olympics. He also was the first Olympian to win the Nobel Peace Prize.

97. What Super Bowl was hosted on January 9 - the earliest date in Super Bowl history?

98. This famous Kansas Citian is a former baseball player who played his entire 21-year career for the Kansas City Royals.

99. What Virginia basketball player won the AP Player of the Year award in 1981, 1982 and 1983?

100. What record setting Miami Dolphins quarterback, who starred in the movie Ace Ventura, never won a Super Bowl?

Answers 91-100

91. Miami Heat

92. John Madden

93. King of Clubs

94. Scottie Pippen

95. Wayne Gretzky

96. Philip Noel-Baker

97. Super Bowl XI

98. George Brett

99. Ralph Sampson

100. Dan Marino

Questions 101-110

101. This WNBA expansion team was added in 1999 along with the Orlando Miracle. 12,122 Minnesotans attended this team's first regular-season game against the Detroit Shock, which they won 68-51.

102. The original colors for this Los Angeles NHL team were purple and gold, the colors of royalty.

103. This famous Arkansan was an Olympic gold medalist in the triple jump (1984). He was also married to Flo-Jo, a multiple Olympic medal-winning sprinter.

104. What left-handed pitcher started for the American League in the 2008 All-Star Game?

105. Who was the MVP of the 1970 MLB All-Star Game despite being on the losing team?

106. What female surfer won the Wolrd Championship six straight years?

107. It's a soccer rivalry between Texas' two MLS teams, the Houston Dynamo and FC Dallas, recognizing the best club in the state for the season.

108. What number did Dale Earnhardt race under when he won the 1980 Winston Cup?

109. What water sport is George Freeth commonly referred to as the father of?

110. Who played 14 seasons as the QB of the New York Giants and was chosen as the MVP of Super Bowl XXI, in which he completed 22 of 25 passes?

Answers 101-110

101. Lynx

102. Kings

103. Al Joyner

104. Cliff Lee

105. Carl Yastrzemski

106. Layne Beachley

107. Texas Derby

108. 2

109. Surfing

110. Phil Simms

Questions 111-120

111. He played from 1890-1905, and finished his career with 75 homeruns. 55 of them the "inside-the-park" variety, which makes him one of the leaders of that feat.

112. What is the name of Alka-Seltzer's mascot?

113. Muhammad Ali used this famous boxing style against George Foreman in 1974's "Rumble in the Jungle," where he would assume a protective stance against the ropes and let his opponent wear himself out by throwing punches.

114. What player set a record for most 3-point shots in an NBA season with 269 during the 2005-2006 season?

115. What NHL team has a giant purple octopus named Al as its unofficial mascot?

116. Which of golf's major championships is held first each year?

117. What team did Eli Manning and the New York Giants beat in their first two Super Bowl appearances?

118. In the 1970 MLB All-Star Game, what outfielder threw the ball to Ray Fosse who attempted to tag Pete Rose out at home plate?

119. What bowling tournament is considered the equivalent of golf's Ryder Cup?

120. How many yards is an offensive holding penalty in the NFL?

Answers 111-120

111. Jesse Burkett

112. Speedy

113. Rope-a-dope

114. Ray Allen

115. Detroit Red Wings

116. The Masters

117. New England Patriots

118. Amos Otis

119. Weber Cup

120. 10

Questions 121-130

121. What state does the Houston Dynamo play its home games in?

122. This MLB team played at the Polo Grounds in New York until the end of the 1957 season, after which it moved to San Francisco.

123. Who tallied over 100 points a season for 14 straight years in the NHL?

124. She became the first athlete to win the Golden Slam of tennis in the same calendar year, winning Olympic gold plus the Grand Slam events in 1988.

125. This figure skater invented a trademark move known as the "Hamill Camel."

126. The Montreal Expos were the first MLB team in Canada, but in 2005 the team moved to Washington, D.C., to become what team?

127. What Hall of Famer started at first base for the National League in the 1973 All-Star Game?

128. What Kansas City Royals' baseball legend required hemorrhoid surgery between games two and three of the 1980 World Series?

129. It's both the name of the rivalry, as well as the trophy awarded to the winner of the regular season series between MLS rivals, D.C. United and New York Red Bulls.

130. What sport did the Newark Peppers play in 1915?

Answers 121-130

121. Texas

122. Giants

123. Wayne Gretzky

124. Steffi Graf

125. Dorothy Hamill

126. Nationals

127. Hank Aaron

128. George Brett

129. Atlantic Cup

130. Baseball

Questions 131-140

131. What sport is divided into periods of time called chukkers?

132. What running back became Super Bowl MVP for the Redskins after capturing their first NFL title since 1942?

133. What number did Peyton Manning wear with the Indianapolis Colts?

134. Along with Alister MacKenzie, this person co-designed Augusta National golf course. Name this golfer who played only as an amateur and retired in 1930 at the age of 28.

135. In 1995, the MLB added two new franchises, one to each league, but decided that having an odd number of teams in each made scheduling difficult. Which team agreed to move from the American to the National League?

136. This NFL team has been playing since 1919, making it the 3rd-oldest franchise in the league. It's fans are known as Cheeseheads.

137. The North American Soccer League (NASL) existed from 1968-1984. The team from Chicago was called?

138. What New York Yankee won the 2002 MLB Home Run Derby?

139. Who did Larry Holmes feel was unable to carry his jockstrap?

140. It's both the name of the rivalry, as well as the trophy awarded to the winner of the regular season series between MLS rivals, D.C. United and New York Red Bulls.

Answers 131-140

131. Polo

132. John Riggins

133. 18

134. Bobby Jones

135. Milwaukee Brewers

136. Green Bay Packers

137. Sting

138. Jason Giambi

139. Rocky Marciano

140. Atlantic Cup

Questions 141-150

141. Phoenix was granted an NBA expansion team in 1968 and, over the years, they've had one of the hottest winning percentages in the league, fitting for a team with this mascot.

142. What boxers participated in the 1975 "Thrilla in Manila" bout?

143. In honor of Ohio's proud Civil War heritage, what did the NHL team from Columbus name itself?

144. Name the traditional form of heavyweight wrestling that has become Japanâ€™s national sport.

145. What stadium hosted the first nighttime World Series game in 1971?

146. It's an annual rivalry between the Columbus Crew and Toronto FC of MLS named after the official flower of Ontario and the official wildflower of Ohio.

147. What European city hosted the 1960 Summer Olympics?

148. It's the trophy awarded to the winner of a college football rivalry game played by the University of Washington Huskies and the Washington State University Cougars.

149. What was the first Super Bowl hosted at the Superdome in New Orleans?

150. What Milwaukee Buck was traded to the Los Angeles Lakers with Kareem Abdul-Jabbar?

Answers 141-150

141. Suns

142. Ali & Frazier

143. Blue Jackets

144. Sumo

145. Three Rivers Stadium

146. Trilliam Cup

147. Rome

148. Apple Cup

149. Super Bowl XII

150. Walt Wesley

Questions 151-160

151. The first world heavyweight champion under the new Marquess of Queensberry Rules was "Gentleman Jim" who defeated John L. Sullivan in 1892. What was Gentleman Jim's last name?

152. Named after the mythical lumberjack Paul Bunyan, what prize is awarded to the winner of the college football game between Minnesota and Wisconsin?

153. This NHL team was created in 1997 as part of a four-team expansion (Atlanta, Columbus, Minnesota, Nashville), in which each would begin play as its new arena was completed. This team from Atlanta began play in 2000.

154. What NBA team did Willis Reed play for when he won the All-Star MVP, the league MVP & Finals MVP in 1970?

155. In 1994, James Orthwein offered Robert Kraft $75 million to pay off the remaining lease at Foxboro Stadium with the intent to move the Patriots to what city?

156. What state does Real Salt Lake play its home games in?

157. What was Dr. J's real name?

158. Which team was the first to score more than 50 points in a Super Bowl when it beat the Denver Broncos 55-10 in Super Bowl XXIV?

159. From 1961-2005, this American golfer won 18 major championships, finished in second place 19 times and third place 9 times, making him one of the most successful golfers of all time.

160. Mayor Bob Lanier refused owner Bud Adams a new NFL stadium after the city had so recently renovated the Astrodome, so Bud moved his team to Memphis in 1997. Two years later, what was the team name changed to?

Answers 151-160

151. Corbett

152. Paul Bunyan's Axe

153. Thrashers

154. Knicks

155. St. Louis

156. Utah

157. Julius Erving

158. San Francisco 49ers

159. Jack Nicklaus

160. Tennessee Titans

Questions 161-170

161. This NHL team was founded in 1972 as the Winnipeg Jets. It moved to Phoenix and assumed this team name on July 1, 1996.

162. In what Canadian city was the 1988 Winter Olympics held?

163. In what place did the Jamaican bobsled team finish at their very first Olympics?

164. What was the average speed at the first Grand Prix race in 1901?

165. What first name should football player Joe Theismann have used when he said, "Nobody in football should be called a genius. A genius is a guy like Norman Einstein?"

166. What Hall of Fame-bound quarterback was reluctantly released by the Indianapolis Colts in 2012 after he missed the entire 2011 season recovering from neck surgery?

167. This famous Kansas Citian is a professional golfer who has played on the PGA Tour and now plays mostly on the Champions Tour. To date, he has won 5 British Opens.

168. This Hall of Fame NBA player attended Indiana State University from 1976-1979, and was then drafted by the Boston Celtics where he played 13 seasons, won three NBA Championships and three league MVP awards.

169. Which NFL team was the first to advance to the Super Bowl in three consecutive years, 1972-1974?

170. Who surpassed "50 goals in 50 games" by his 39th game of the 1981-82 season?

Answers 161-170

161. Coyotes

162. Calgary

163. Last

164. 46 Mph

165. Albert

166. Peyton Manning

167. Tom Watson

168. Larry Bird

169. Miami Dolphins

170. Wayne Gretzky

Questions 171-180

171. Who was the first player in the National League to hit two grand slams in the same game?

172. How many feet are horseshoe stakes traditionally set apart?

173. This NBA franchise began in 1974 in New Orleans, but 1979 moved to Utah after five seasons. Not exactly a musical Mecca, I must say.

174. This coach, known as "The Big Tuna," was famously quoted when he left the Patriots in 1996, "If they want you to cook the dinner; at least they ought to let you shop for some of the groceries." Name him!

175. It's a college football rivalry game between played by the Mississippi State Bulldogs and University of Mississippi Rebels.

176. This maple-flavored oatmeal cereal had Mickey Mantle crying, "I want my _____!"

177. This name for Indiana's NBA team is derived from the speed-limiting car in the Indianapolis 500.

178. San Francisco named their NFL team for the year these gold rush miners and prospectors.

179. What company introduced player statistics to baseball cards in 1952?

180. What university played the University of Chicago in the first men's college basketball game in 1896?

Answers 171-180

171. Tony Cloninger

172. 40

173. Jazz

174. Bill Parcells

175. Egg Bowl

176. Maypo

177. Pacers

178. 49ers

179. Topps

180. University of Iowa

Questions 181-190

181. In what Austrian city were the 1964 Winter Olympics held?

182. It's a college football rivalry between the Auburn University Tigers and the University of Georgia Bulldogs.

183. What is the only Major Tom Watson has not won?

184. What billiards game is a slang term for a first-year cadet in the British army?

185. How many Super Bowls did the Denver Broncos lose before finally winning Super Bowl XXXII?

186. Until they gained a Major League Soccer team in 2011, this NBA team was the only major league franchise in Portland, Oregon.

187. What was the first NFL team to advance to the Super Bowl in three consecutive years?

188. What boxers were involved in the controversial "long count" bout of 1927?

189. This famous Arkansan is a former football coach who became only the second coach to win both an NCAA Championship and an NFL Championship (1995, Dallas Cowboys).

190. After being accused of stealing players from other teams, the Pittsburgh Alleghenys changed their name to this current Pittsburgh MLB team?

Answers 181-190

181. Innsbruck

182. Deep South's Oldest Rivalry

183. PGA

184. Snooker

185. 3

186. Trailblazers

187. Miami Dolphins

188. Dempsey & Tunney

189. Barry Switzer

190. Pirates

Questions 191-200

191. What province do the Vancouver Whitecaps play their home games in?

192. What New York Yankee won the 2011 MLB Home Run Derby?

193. There are two NHL teams in New York, but only one of them plays in Madison Square Garden. Which one?

194. Which professional sports league features the teams the Toronto Argonauts, the Winnipeg Blue Bombers & the Saskatchewan Roughriders?

195. What event did Joan Benoit win at the 1984 Los Angeles Olympics?

196. Who was the first hockey player to break the 200-point mark in a season?

197. How many games did the Chicago Bulls lose in the 1995-1996 season?

198. What was Sam Snead's nickname?

199. What team was Wade Boggs playing for when he got his 3000th career hit?

200. What Philadelphia Phillie won the 2005 MLB Home Run Derby?

Answers 191-200

191. British Columbia

192. Robinson Cano

193. Rangers

194. CFL

195. Marathon

196. Wayne Gretzky

197. 10

198. Slammin' Sammy

199. Tampa Bay Devil Rays

200. Bobby Abreau

Questions 201-210

201. It's a soccer trophy awarded to the yearly winner of the rivalry between two MLS teams, Real Salt Lake and the Colorado Rapids.

202. What sport's origins come from the Native American sport of baggataway?

203. This MLB pitcher was an eight-time MLB All-Star who amassed 5,714 career strikeouts, first in baseball history by 839 strikeouts over Randy Johnson.

204. Who was the first Spaniard to win one of golf's major championships? He did so by winning the British Open in 1979.

205. Who was the first NCAA basketball player to win the AP Player of the Year award in 1961?

206. This football team was founded in 1959 when minor league baseball owner Bob Howsam was awarded an AFL charter franchise. In 1983, they acquired John Elway, who swore he would play baseball instead of play for the Colts.

207. The Minnesota Twins MLB franchise originally was named what team from 1901-1960?

208. In 2007, this Major League Soccer team confirmed that David Beckham would be leaving the soccer powerhouse Real Madrid to begin a professional stint in the States.

209. Baseball is 90% mental and the other half is what, according to Yogi Berra?

210. This Major League Baseball player was nicknamed "The Georgia Peach."

Answers 201-210

201. Rocky Mountain Cup

202. Lacrosse

203. Nolan Ryan

204. Seve Ballesteros

205. Jerry Lucas

206. Broncos

207. Washington Senators

208. Los Angeles Galaxy

209. Physical

210. Ty Cobb

Questions 211-220

211. What position did Tony Cloninger play when he hit two grand slams in the same game?

212. Selected in the fifth round of the 1975 NFL Draft, what Kansas State University QB played his entire NFL career with the New England Patriots until retiring in 1990?

213. What was thrown for a record 98.48 meters by Jan Zelezny in 1996?

214. Because he refused to play for the Chargers, what QB was immediately traded to the New York Giants in 2004 for draft picks and Philip Rivers?

215. What University of Kansas football player helped the Jayhawks win a 1960 game over #1-ranked Missouri, but was later declared ineligible due to a recruiting violation?

216. What NFL team has a pack of rapid fans known as the Dawg Pound?

217. What category is represented by orange in the original "Trivial Pursuit?"

218. Detroit's MLB team took its name from this Detroit Light Guard, they fought ferociously during the Civil War.

219. Who is the only heavyweight boxer to be World Champion from a disqualification?

220. In 1896, upon learning that the Olympic discus was only 2kg rather than 10kg, this American entered the event and won.

Answers 211-220

211. Pitcher

212. Steve Grogan

213. Javelin

214. Eli Manning

215. Bert Coan

216. Cleveland Browns

217. Sports & Leisure

218. Tigers

219. Max Schmeling

220. Robert Garrett

Questions 221-230

221. This German Formula One racing driver is widely regarded as the greatest F1 driver of all time on his performance records alone. He's won seven World Championships.

222. This famous Arkansan is a professional baseball player who has been known to climb the fence and take away home runs. The Twins selected him in the first round in 1993.

223. This famous Kansas Citian spent 14 years playing in the NBA, most notably with the Kansas City Kings and Boston Celtics. His nickname was "Tiny."

224. Who was the first female Olympic athlete to appear on a Wheaties cereal box?

225. This MLB team was founded as the Brown Stockings in 1882 as part of the American Association.

226. A set of rules were drafted for the amateur boxing championships held at Lillie Bridge in London in 1867, named for the patronage of the Marquess of what?

227. Fans of this MLB team from Atlanta, GA, have adopted the Tomahawk Chop to rally the home team at their games.

228. The North American Soccer League (NASL) existed from 1968-1984. The team from Seattle was called?

229. What month is The Masters held?

230. What team did Lynette Woodward play for when she became the team's first woman player?

Answers 221-230

221. Michael Schumacher

222. Torii Hunter

223. Nate Archibald

224. Mary Lou Retton

225. St. Louis Cardinals

226. Queensberry

227. Braves

228. Sounders

229. April

230. Harlem Globetrotters

Questions 231-240

231. Named for the Spanish Franciscan friars who founded San Diego in 1769, what is the name of San Diego's MLB team?

232. The 1947 World Series between the New York Yankees and the Brooklyn Dodgers was not only the first to be televised, it was also the first Series to involve an African-American player. Who was he?

233. Though one might expect to find them in Ancient Rome, Ottawa is actually home to this group of NHLers?

234. This MLB player hit 24 or more home runs every year from 1955-1973, including 30 or more home runs in a season at least fifteen times. He retired with 755 career homeruns.

235. The Cincinnati Zoo was home to a rare white one, which prompted Paul Brown to name the Cincinnati NFL team this in 1967.

236. What was the first year the World Series was broadcast in color?

237. It's a soccer trophy awarded to the yearly winner of the rivalry between two MLS teams, Real Salt Lake and the Colorado Rapids.

238. In what French city were the 1968 Winter Olympics held?

239. What golf course names its holes after characters from the book "Treasure Island?"

240. It's an intercollegiate rivalry between The University of New Mexico and New Mexico State University that began in 1894.

Answers 231-240

231. Padres

232. Jackie Robinson

233. Senators

234. Hank Aaron

235. Bengals

236. 1954

237. Rocky Mountain Cup

238. Grenoble

239. Spyglass Hill

240. Rio Grande Rivalry

Questions 241-250

241. This Major League Baseball player was nicknamed "The Rocket."

242. On May 10th, 1999, who became the first player in baseball history to hit two grand slams on his home field?

243. Prior to this NHL team's first season in 1967, Pittsburgh had been the home of the NHL's Pirates (1925-1932) and the AHL's Hornets from the 1930s to the 1960s.

244. It's a college football rivalry game played by the Oregon Ducks and the Washington Huskies.

245. What sport officially replaced its 38mm balls with 40mm balls in 2000?

246. At what race was Dale Earnhardt killed in 2001?

247. In 2000, what San Francisco 49ers wide receiver ran to midfield after a touchdown and controversially spiked the ball on the Dallas Cowboys' star?

248. At one point in their past, this New York NFL team was called "The Big Blue Wrecking Crew" for their crushing defensive line.

249. What player set a record for most three-point shots in an NBA season with 269 during the 2005-2006 season?

250. What team beat the Dallas Cowboys to win the "Ice Bowl"?

Answers 241-250

241. Roger Clemens

242. Nomar Garciaparra

243. Penguins

244. Border War

245. Table Tennis

246. Daytona 500

247. Terrell Owens

248. Giants

249. Ray Allen

250. Green Bay Packers

Questions 251-260

251. What team is most well known for the "Sausage Race" at the bottom of the sixth inning?

252. What yacht club won the America's Cup 25 straight times?

253. In Major League Baseball, what is the baseline distance between bases?

254. At the 1996 Atlanta Summer Olympics, Hong Kong (as a British colony) athlete Lee Lai Shan won his country's first-ever gold medal in this sport. He received it in the Mistral One Design event.

255. He was the U.S. national team goalkeeper for the 1990 and 1994 World Cups, nearly helping his team beat Brazil in the second round in 1994.

256. Ken Burns based his 2005 documentary "Unforgivable Blackness" on the rise and fall of this boxer, who in 1910 became the first black heavyweight champion.

257. What was Secretariat's nickname?

258. In the first ever Super Bowl (III) to actually bear the name "Super Bowl," what quarterback guaranteed victory and then pulled off one of the greatest upsets of all time?

259. What kind of sporting events are held at Frontier Days in Cheyenne, Wyoming; The Roundup in Pendleton, Oregon; and The Stampede in Calgary, Alberta?

260. What day of the week is the Old Course at St. Andrews closed to golf?

Answers 251-260

251. Milwaukee Brewers

252. New York Yacht Club

253. 90 Feet

254. Sailing

255. Tony Meola

256. Jack Johnson

257. Big Red

258. Joe Namath

259. Rodeos

260. Sunday

Questions 261-270

261. This Detroit Tigers pitcher lost his perfect game in 2010, when first-base umpire Jim Joyce mistakenly called the last batter safe on an infield single. Name this pitcher.

262. In 1952, Sugar Ray Robinson donated all but $1 of his prize money for the heavyweight championship to the Cancer Fund of this writer, whose short stories were the inspiration for the Broadway musical Guys and Dolls.

263. In 1938, what tennis star won the French, Wimbledon, U.S. and Australian Championships to become the first person to win the grand slam?

264. What sport did Anders Haugen receive a bronze medal for 50 years after he competed in the 1924 Winter Olympics when a scoring error was discovered in 1974?

265. What year saw the bottom of the net opened so the ball could flow through in basketball?

266. What University of Kansas football player helped the Jayhawks win a 1960 game over #1-ranked Missouri, but was later declared ineligible due to a recruiting violation?

267. During the 1995 Masters Tournament, this professional golfer-turned-broadcaster said that the 17th green was so fast that it seemed to be bikini-waxed.

268. Who was the third overall pick in the 1984 NBA draft?

269. What hockey star met his wife when he was a judge on "Dance Fever" in 1984?

270. This event made its Olympic debut at the 2000 Sydney Summer Olympics. It was won by Brigitte McMahon from Switzerland.

Answers 261-270

261. Armando Galarraga

262. Damon Runyan

263. Don Budge

264. Ski Jumping

265. 1913

266. Bert Coan

267. Gary McCord

268. Michael Jordan

269. Wayne Gretzky

270. Triathlon

Questions 271-280

271. What Los Angeles Angels of Anaheim player won the 2007 MLB Home Run Derby?

272. He's one of the youngest players to ever to hit 500 homeruns, breaking the record set in 1939 by Jimmie Foxx.

273. What team did John Madden coach for in the NFL?

274. Companion to the Washington Wizards of the NBA, this WNBA team based in Washington, D.C., which began play as an expansion team in 1998 is called?

275. What state do the Colorado Rapids play their home games in?

276. What team's "Doomsday Defense" did not allow the Miami Dolphins to score a touchdown in Super Bowl VI?

277. In 1966, the MLB's Braves moved to Atlanta from what city?

278. What was the collective nickname for these 1980s New York Giants linebackers (Carson, Kelley, Taylor, Van Pelt) known for their bone-jarring tackles?

279. What ABA star sank the most 3-point shots in a season with 199 in the 1968-1969 season?

280. What sport features slang terms such as "worm burners" and "chili dippers?"

Answers 271-280

271. Vladimir Guerrero

272. Alex Rodriguez

273. Oakland Raiders

274. Mystics

275. Colorado

276. Cowboys

277. Milwaukee

278. Crunch Bunch

279. Louie Dampier

280. Golf

Questions 281-290

281. When this NHL team moved to Carolina from Hartford, it changed its colors and name to this more weather-related mascot.

282. This NFL team has played in Kansas City, Missouri, since it left Dallas in 1963 where it was called the Dallas Texans.

283. What NBA coach had an astounding .688 winning percentage when he retired?

284. Harold Toshiyuki Sakata, silver medalist in wrestling at the 1948 Olympics, later appeared as this villian in a James Bond film.

285. What city hosted the NCAA Men's Basketball Final Four games from 1943 to 1948?

286. To be considered this weight class, a boxer must not exceed 147 lbs.

287. It's the rivalry between two MLS teams, San Jose Earthquakes and L.A. Galaxy, which many believe to be the fiercest in American soccer.

288. How many yards deep is the endzone in the NFL?

289. It's an annual cup awarded to the winner of the regular season series between MLS teams, San Jose Earthquakes and Seattle Sounders, named after the NASL predecessors.

290. What Milwaukee Brewer won the 2009 MLB Home Run Derby?

Answers 281-290

281. Hurricanes

282. Chiefs

283. Phil Jackson

284. Odd Job

285. New York City

286. Welterweight

287. California Clasico

288. 10

289. Heritage Cup

290. Prince Fielder

Questions 291-300

291. What number did Peyton Manning wear for the Indianapolis Colts?

292. What state do the San Jose Earthquakes play they home games in?

293. What was the first year the NHL permitted professional players to compete in ice hockey at the Winter Olympics? These games took place in Nagano, Japan.

294. Who beat Magic Johnson for Rookie of the Year honors in the 1979-1980 season?

295. The Big Apple was first popularized as a reference to New York City by John J. Fitz Gerald in a number of New York Morning Telegraph articles in the 1920s in reference to what New York sport?

296. At the 2000 Sydney Summer Olympics, favored Spain lost the soccer final in a penalty shootout, 5-3, to this nation.

297. One area of the water near the San Francisco Bay Area is known as the "Red Triangle" because of the proliferation of this animal, which also lends its name to San Jose's NHL team.

298. The United Soccer League's Puerto Rico team and one of the New York NHL teams both share what mascot?

299. Familiar to crossword enthusiasts, this 3-letter word is one of the 4 main punches in boxing: when the leading fist thrown from a boxing stance straight ahead and fully extended at the opponent.

300. Who scored the first TD in Super Bowl history with a 37-yard reception against the Kansas City Chiefs?

Answers 291-300

291. 18

292. California

293. 1998

294. Larry Bird

295. Horse Racing

296. Cameroon

297. Sharks

298. Islanders

299. Jab

300. Max McGee

Questions 301-310

301. In 1937, the NFL's Boston Braves moved their stadium from Braves Field to Fenway Park. What did they rename the team?

302. Windsurfer Gal Fridman won this country's first-ever gold medal at the 2004 Athens Summer Olympics.

303. This network has televised The Masters since 1956. Prior to 1933, it only televised the final four holes.

304. Before moving to Los Angeles and becoming arguably one of the greatest NBA franchises of all time, this team was located in Minnesota.

305. Established in 1881 as an independent team, Cincinnati's MLB team is one of the oldest major league clubs to have played continuously in one city.

306. What year did the Dodgers move from Brooklyn to Los Angeles?

307. This NFL team was the first to have an official marching band and the first to have a fight song, "Hail to the..."

308. What Celtic made the first three-point shot in the NBA against the Houston Rockets on October 12, 1979 with 3:48 left in the first quarter?

309. How far is a Major League Baseball baserunner allowed to stray from his baseline in an attempt to avoid a tag?

310. Who scored the first touchdown in Super Bowl history with a 37 yard reception against the Kansas City Chiefs?

Answers 301-310

301. Boston Redskins

302. Israel

303. CBS

304. Lakers

305. Reds

306. 1958

307. Redskins

308. Chris Ford

309. 3 Feet

310. Max McGee

Questions 311-320

311. This Major League Soccer team based in Washington, D.C., was among the first ten teams in the league. It also played in the inaugural match on April 6, 1996, losing to the San Jose Clash 1-0.

312. What team won five World Series titles from 1903 through 1918?

313. What player, nicknamed "The Admiral," recorded a quadruple-double against the Detroit Pistons in 1994?

314. On August 9, 2010, the San Francisco Giants hosted a tribute night in which an ensemble of 9000 kazoo players attempted a rendition of what popular ballpark theme?

315. What is the most popular type of fish sought after by fly fisherman?

316. The North American Soccer League (NASL) existed from 1968-1984. The team from Kansas City was called?

317. In 1919, this Senators pitcher retired 28 Yankee batters in a row. Name this Hall of Fame player who was nicknamed "The Big Train."

318. After how many points do players alternate serves in 21-point table tennis?

319. This NHL team won its fourth Stanley Cup in 2010 by defeating the Philadelphia Flyers in the best-of-seven series 4-2.

320. How many years did the New York Yacht Club hold the America's Cup until "Australia II" defeated Dennis Conner's "Liberty" in 1983?

Answers 311-320

311. United

312. Boston Red Sox

313. David Robinson

314. Take Me Out to the Ballgame

315. Trout

316. Spurs

317. Walter Johnson

318. 5

319. Blackhawks

320. 132

Questions 321-330

321. What year did the New York Yacht Club win the America's Cup for the first time?

322. Pete Mitchell from the 1986 film "Top Gun" would likely approve of this NBA team from Dallas, TX.

323. Counting the two green "house" numbers 0 and 00 (double zero), how many numbers are on an American roulette wheel?

324. What Celtic made the first 3-point shot in the NBA against the Houston Rockets on October 12, 1979, with 3:48 left in the first quarter?

325. What Boston Red Sox player won the 2010 MLB Home Run Derby?

326. What bar sport was banned in Florida in 1989?

327. When he retired in 1999, this Australian wicket-keeper held the world record for most Test dismissals at 395.

328. He started the final round of the 2012 British Open six shots behind leader Adam Scott, who bogeyed the last four holes to give this golfer his second Claret Jug and fourth major.

329. Who became an honorary member of the Harlem Globetrotters in 1976?

330. Who played in the most NBA games in league history?

Answers 321-330

321. 1851

322. Mavericks

323. 38

324. Chris Ford

325. David Ortiz

326. Dwarf Tossing

327. Ian Healy

328. Ernie Els

329. Henry Kissinger

330. Robert Parish

Questions 331-340

331. The North American Soccer League (NASL) existed from 1968-1984. The team from Los Angeles was called?

332. The Missouri-Kansas college football rivalry, which began on October 31, 1891, is one of the oldest such rivalries west of what river?

333. The 1985 Chicago Bears were one of the greatest teams in the history of the NFL. In Super Bowl XX they set records for most sacks (7) & fewest rushing yards allowed (7) against what team?

334. What province does the Montreal Impact play its home games in?

335. What country hosted the 2002 Winter Olympics?

336. This Dodger lefty was inducted into the Baseball Hall of Fame in 1972. Name this pitcher who was the first to pitch four no-hitters, including a perfect game in 1965.

337. What Tarheel won the AP Player of the Year award in basketball in 1984?

338. The Seattle Reign preceded this WNBA team as a charter member of the American Basketball League. When the Reign fell in 1998, Seattle was quickly awarded a WNBA franchise that began playing under this name in 2000.

339. Rally Fries are a baseball tradition started by this Seattle-based MLB team's broadcaster Mike Blowers in 2007 when a fan trying to catch a foul ball reached over the wall and spilled his french fries on the warning track.

340. What sport has a three-sided court called a fronton?

Answers 331-340

331. Aztecs

332. Mississippi

333. Patriots

334. Quebec

335. USA

336. Sandy Koufax

337. Michael Jordan

338. Storm

339. Mariners

340. Jai Alai

Questions 341-350

341. In 2006, the San Jose Earthquakes owners, players and a few coaches moved to Houston, Texas, to become the what MLS expansion team?

342. What kicker--one of the most accurate ever--played 13 seasons with the Ravens & was inducted to the team's "Ring of Honor"Â in 2011?

343. Who was the first quarterback the Indianapolis Colts signed after releasing Peyton Manning?

344. What figure skater and silver medal winner at the 1994 Winter Olympics told Mickey Mouse, "This is the most corniest thing I have ever done," during a parade at Disney World?

345. In 2007, this Tampa Bay MLB team changed its mascot from the marine animal that killed Steve Irwin to this representation of a beam of sunlight.

346. The North American Soccer League (NASL) existed from 1968-1984. The team from Rochester was called?

347. What Kansas City Royals player was accidentally printed on Juan LeBron's 1995 Topps Traded and Rookie baseball card (#12T)?

348. He pitched for the KC and Oakland Athletics from 1965-1974, and became the highest paid pitcher in baseball when he signed with the Yankees in 1975. Name this man.

349. Although Art Modell moved the Ravens from this city in 1996, the team's history and archives remained behind. What city did the Ravens leave?

350. Alternately called "The Bronx Bombers" by fans and "The Evil Empire" by detractors, this is the name of the American League MLB team from New York.

Answers 341-350

341. Dynamo

342. Matt Stover

343. Trevor Vittatoe

344. Nancy Kerrigan

345. Rays

346. Lancers

347. Carlos Beltran

348. Catfish Hunter

349. Cleveland

350. Yankees

Questions 351-360

351. What golfer gave advice such as, "Keep close count of your nickels and dimes, stay away from whiskey, and never concede a putt?"

352. How many touchdowns did Peyton Manning throw in the 2004 season?

353. What surfer was named World Champion for a record seventh time in 2005?

354. How old was Tiger Woods when he won his first Masters Green Jacket in 1997?

355. In what state was golfing bad boy John Daly born?

356. What make of car won the first Daytona 500?

357. It's the name of the trophy awarded each year to the best MLS team in the Pacific Northwest between the Portland Timbers, Seattle Sounders & Vancouver Whitecaps.

358. What state does FC Dallas play its home games in?

359. What province does Toronto FC play its home game in?

360. What team started as the Boston Red Stockings in 1871?

Answers 351-360

351. Sam Snead

352. 49

353. Kelly Slater

354. 21

355. California

356. Oldsmobile

357. Cascadia Cup

358. Texas

359. Ontario

360. Atlanta Braves

Questions 361-370

361. Major League Soccer was founded in 1993 as part of the United States' bid to host what international event in 1994?

362. This famous Arkansan is a retired professional basketball player who, while in college, led the Razorbacks "The Triplets" to the 1978 Final Four. His nickname was "Sid the Squid."

363. This NBA player is the league's all-time leading scorer with 38,387 points. From 1969-1989, he won six NBA championships and six regular season MVP Awards.

364. What ancient tradition did French educator Baron Pierre de Coubertin propose reviving in 1894?

365. What professional sport do the Philadelphia Wings, Rochester Knighthawks, Calgary Roughnecks & Minnesota Swarm compete in?

366. This NBA player was three-point sharp-shooter during his 18-year career as an Indiana Pacer. In fact, his nickname was "Knick Killer." He once made three-pointers in 68 consecutive games.

367. What team did Fernando Tatis play for when he hit two grand slams in one inning in 2011?

368. The North American Soccer League (NASL) existed from 1968-1984. The team from Washington was called?

369. At the 2004 Athens Summer Olympics, this country won its first-ever gold medals with wins in men's tennis singles and doubles.

370. What pitcher started for the National League in the 2008 All-Star Game, then filed for free agency at end of the season?

Answers 361-370

361. World Cup

362. Sidney Moncrief

363. Kareem Abdul-Jabbar

364. Olympic Games

365. Lacrosse

366. Reggie Miller

367. St. Louis Cardinals

368. Darts

369. Chile

370. Ben Sheets

Questions 371-380

371. 118 lbs. is the maximum weight for a fighter in what weight class?

372. Which country did the U.S. defeat in ice hockey for the gold medal at the 1980 Lake Placid Olympics?

373. On October 26, 1993, NFL owners voted to add this Carolina-based team as the 29th franchise, the first new team added to the league since 1976.

374. Floyd Patterson held the record for youngest heavyweight champion until 1986 when this boxer scored a TKO against Trevor Berbick at the age of 20.

375. Houston's Major League Soccer team shares its name with one of the murderous gladiators from the movie "The Running Man." Which one?

376. This famous Arkansan is a professional golfer known primarily for his driving distance off the tee, which earned him the nickname "Long John."

377. Who did Wilt Chamberlain score 100 points against in an NBA game in 1962?

378. This famous Arkansan was a college football player and coach who amassed 6 national championships and 13 conference championships during his 25-year stint at Alabama.

379. This NBA team was established in 1993 when the NBA expanded into Canada by awarding Toronto businessman John Bitove a team for an expansion fee of US$125 million.

380. What New Jersey NHL team takes its name from the legend of the mythological monster that roams the Pine Barrens of New Jersey?

Answers 371-380

371. Bantamweight

372. Finland

373. Panthers

374. Mike Tyson

375. Dynamo

376. John Daly

377. New York Knickerbockers

378. Paul "Bear" Bryant

379. Raptors

380. Devils

Questions 381-390

381. Which Dallas-based professional football team does Jerry Jones own?

382. Toss a telephone pole up in the air and it will hopefully perform a 180-degree turn landing with the end you were holding sticking in the air. What is this sport, which is frequently part of Scottish festivals?

383. After playing for the 1984 U.S. Olympic team, he was drafted tenth overall by the Oakland A's in the 1984 MLB draft. Name this man who hit 33 homeruns before the 1987 All-Star break.

384. How many innings did it take the Houston Astros to defeat the Atlanta Braves in a 2005 playoff game?

385. How many pins are on the back row in American bowling?

386. Where is the only place the libero may play in volleyball?

387. This famous Arkansan is a professional baseball pitcher who recorded a no-hitter in a complete game shutout against the San Diego Padres on May 12, 2001.

388. in 2001, this team became the fastest expansion team in the MLB to win a World Series, doing it in only the fourth season since their expansion in 1998.

389. In 2012, this cyclist became the first winner of the Tour de France to hail from Great Britain in the 99-year history of the race.

390. Some boxing federations refer to them as Junior Heavyweights, but most refer to boxers who are in the weight class just below heavyweights by this term.

Answers 381-390

381. Cowboys

382. Caber Tossing

383. Mark McGwire

384. 18

385. 4

386. Back Row

387. A.J. Burnett

388. Arizona Diamondbacks

389. Bradley Wiggins

390. Cruiserweight

Questions 391-400

391. What baseball player disappeared in a plane crash off the coast of San Juan, Puerto Rico, on New Year's Eve in 1972?

392. Norm Sloan coached what college basketball team to a 30-1 record and a national title in 1974?

393. How many balls are used in the pocket billiards game eight ball?

394. Who did Mohammad Ali defeat using the rope-a-dope strategy in the bout titled "The Rumble in the Jungle"?

395. Chicago's "Lovable Losers" have held one of the longest streaks without a championship in North American professional sports at more than 100 years. Is it due to The Curse of the Billy Goat?

396. What team "earned" the right to pick first in the 2012 NFL Draft by finishing a dismal 2-14 in the 2011 season?

397. What team did Chuck Howley play for when he became the first defensive player to be named 1970 Super Bowl MVP? His team lost to the Colts.

398. This NFL quarterback was drafted by the Steelers in the first round of the 2004 NFL Draft. He played college football at Miami University.

399. These coaches were on the short-list to be the first coach for this Jacksonville NFL franchise: Mike Shanahan, Tony Dungy and Tom Coughlin. Ultimately, all three went on to win Super Bowls, but not for Jacksonville.

400. Who won his first Green Jacket when he won the 2011 Masters Tournament?

Answers 391-400

391. Roberto Clemente

392. North Carolina State

393. 16

394. George Foreman

395. Cubs

396. Indianapolis Colts

397. Cowboys

398. Ben Roethlisberger

399. Jaguars

400. Charl Schwartzel

Questions 401-410

401. Who was the first baseball player to have his name branded into a Louisville Slugger bat?

402. What team sport made its official Olympic debut at the 1920 Summer Olympics in Antwerp, Belgium?

403. The New England area is home to this Major League Soccer team that's named in homage to the Colonial battles that took place there.

404. How many MVP awards did Bill Russell win his career?

405. In 1947, he was the only heavyweight champion in history to retire with an undefeated record.

406. After Super Bowl XLVI, which Manning, at least temperarily, owns the bragging rights to the most Super Bowls rings?

407. Which athlete was repeatedly bumped by Zola Budd during the women's 3000m run at the 1984 Los Angeles Olympics?

408. What hockey legend was traded to the L.A. Kings in 1988?

409. What team was the first to score more than 40 points in a Super Bowl when it beat the New England Patriots 46-10 on January 26, 1986?

410. What stadium hosted the first night World Series game in 1971?

Answers 401-410

401. Honus Wagner

402. Ice Hockey

403. Revolution

404. 5

405. Rocky Marciano

406. Eli Manning

407. Mary Decker

408. Wayne Gretzky

409. Chicago Bears

410. Three Rivers Stadium

Questions 411-420

411. In 1997, which team became the first-ever wild card team to win the World Series?

412. In Super Bowl XXXV, the Ravens defense recorded four sacks, forced five turnovers and allowed only 152 yards, largely due to this eventual MVP of the game.

413. Before moving to St. Louis in 1995, this NFL team played in Cleveland, Los Angeles and Anaheim from 1936-1994.

414. This NFL team originated as the Boston Braves in 1932. It relocated to Washington, D.C., in 1937, and changed its name to this modern day team.

415. What was the first year the Super Bowl was hosted in February?

416. What annual international bicycle race lasts 3 weeks and covers 3,600 km?

417. Who introduced the football helmet?

418. Though there are several teams with this mascot, only this NBA team from Chicago had Michael Jordan.

419. Who did Coach Muzz MacPherson suggest wear number 99?

420. It's the name of the trophy awarded each year to the best MLS team in the Pacific Northwest between the Portland Timbers, Seattle Sounders and Vancouver Whitecaps.

Answers 411-420

411. Florida Marlins

412. Ray Lewis

413. Rams

414. Redskins

415. 2002

416. Tour de France

417. James Naismith

418. Bulls

419. Wayne Gretzky

420. Cascadia Cup

Questions 421-430

421. What team did Neal Ball play for when he made an unassisted triple play against the Boston Red Sox on July 19, 1909?

422. What district does D.C. United play its home games in?

423. What minor league baseball team was Atlanta's home team until they were replaced by the Braves in 1966?

424. The Philadelphia Eagles first Super Bowl loss in 1981 allowed what team to be the first wild card to ever win a Super Bowl?

425. The 2006 FIFA World Cup finals were held in what country? The visitors were probably greeted with the word, "Willkommen!"

426. Who has been the Dodger's play-by-play announcer for 55 years?

427. Confident that the MLB would return a baseball team to Seattle within a few years after the Pilots left, the county built the Kingdome. And, in 1977 this team played their first game there.

428. What year did the Charlotte Hornets move to New Orleans?

429. It's a college football rivalry game played by the Virginia Cavaliers and the North Carolina Tar Heels.

430. This nation won its first ever Olympic medal competing in Shooting (men's double trap) at the 2000 Summer Olympics.

Answers 421-430

421. Indians

422. Columbia

423. Crackers

424. Oakland Raiders

425. Germany

426. Vin Scully

427. Mariners

428. 2002

429. South's Oldest Rivalry

430. Kuwait

Questions 431-440

431. He holds the major league record with 688 intentional walks. Name this 8-time Gold Glove winner, 7-time National League MVP and alleged steroid user.

432. This NBA team in Cleveland shares its name with a model of automobile produced by Chevrolet.

433. What team did Chuck Howley play for when he became the first defensive player to be name Super Bowl MVP?

434. It was originally called the 100 Guinea Cup; a race around Isle of Wight that began in 1851.

435. In 1969, this player became the first Kansas City Royal selected to the MLB All-Star team.

436. Who retired from the Chicago Bulls in 1993, and again in 1999?

437. In 1935, he hit golf's "Shot Heard 'Round the World" by holing out a double eagle on the par 5 fifteenth hole at The Masters. Name this golfer nicknamed "The Squire," a winner of the Career Grand Slam.

438. Down 27-21 to the Cowboys in the NFC Championship, Montana lofted the ball to Clark in the end zone for a TD. What has this play been nicknamed?

439. What Alan Parsons Project song frequently announced the 1990s-era Chicago Bulls?

440. Yuriy Sedykh set a world record of 86.74m in this event at the 1986 Stuttgart Olympic Games. Modern competitions involve a heavy metal ball attached to a wire and handle.

Answers 431-440

431. Barry Bonds

432. Cavaliers

433. Dallas Cowboys

434. America's Cup

435. Ellie Rodriguez

436. Michael Jordan

437. Gene Sarazen

438. The Catch

439. Sirius

440. Hammer Throw

Questions 441-450

441. What was the name of the schooner that won the America's Cup for the New York Club the very first time?

442. In 2008, this player was the first Canadian to win a MLB Home Run Derby?

443. This 1999 expansion team to the WNBA played its first four season in Orlando as the Orlando Miracle before moving to Connecticut in 2003 and changing its name to this moniker.

444. What team did Brett Favre play for in his final NFL season ... maybe?

445. At the 1996 Atlanta Summer Olympics, she became the first American female athlete in history to win four gold medals in a single Olympic games.

446. This 6'11" Detroit Pistons center from Boston, MA, was a four-time All-Star and a vital part, especially for his rebounding skill, of the team that won NBA championships in 1989 and 1990.

447. Who was the first overall draft pick in the 1969 NBA draft?

448. He made his major league debut in 1954 for the Washington Senators, and finished his career 22 years later with 573 homeruns. Name this player nicknamed "The Killer."

449. The North American Soccer League (NASL) existed from 1968-1984. The team from Dallas was called?

450. What team did Barry Bonds play for when he left baseball in 2007?

Answers 441-450

441. America

442. Justin Morneau

443. Sun

444. Minnesota Vikings

445. Amy Van Dyken

446. Bill Laimbeer

447. Kareem Abdul-Jabbar

448. Harmon Killebrew

449. Tornado

450. San Francisco Giants

Questions 451-460

451. Who was the first African-American Major League baseball player?

452. What player has the most cumulative points in NBA All-Star Game history, finally surpassing Michael Jordan in 2012?

453. It's a college rivalry between the sports teams of the South Carolina Gamecocks and the Clemson Tigers.

454. Who won the first four WNBA Finals MVP awards?

455. When they were in New York, this team won 5 World Series Championships and 17 Pennants, but once they moved to San Francisco what MLB team didn't win another championship until 2010?

456. In what city did the first Olympic torch relay end after 3,330 runners carried it through Greece, Bulgaria, Yugoslavia, Hungary, Austria, Czechoslovakia & Germany?

457. What sport involves brassies, spoons, mid-mashies, mashie niblicks, birdies, mulligans and pitching wedges?

458. Who was the first NBA player to win three MVP awards in a row?

459. Who won the 2003 and 2004 Madden Bowl?

460. At the first modern Olympics in 1896, what was awarded to the winner of each event?

Answers 451-460

451. Jackie Robinson

452. Kobe Bryant

453. Battle of the Palmetto State

454. Cynthia Cooper

455. Giants

456. Berlin

457. Golf

458. Bill Russell

459. Dwight Freeney

460. Silver Medal

Questions 461-470

461. After winning a gold medal at the 1920 Summer Olympics for boxing, what sport did Eddie Eagan win a gold medal for at the 1932 Winter Olympics?

462. It's a college football rivalry game played by the Utah Utes and the Utah State Aggies.

463. This famous Arkansan is a former professional baseball player for the Baltimore Orioles (1955-1977) nicknamed "The Human Vacuum Cleaner."

464. Bango has been the official mascot for Milwaukee's NBA team since his debut in at the beginning of the 1977 season. What NBA team plays in Milwaukee, Wisconsin?

465. What team won the first four WNBA titles?

466. Also known as "The Open Championship," this tournament is the oldest of the four major championships in professional golf.

467. This Canadian MLB team came into existence in 1976 along with the Seattle Mariners, as one of two teams added to the American League.

468. On July 12th, 2003, who became the first player in baseball history to hit two grand slams, one from each side of the plate, in the same game?

469. This WNBA team from New York has made it to the league finals in 1997, 1999, 2000 and 2002, losing to the Houston Comets three times and the Los Angeles Sparks once.

470. What baseball team was Dan Marino drafted by before deciding to play football?

Answers 461-470

461. Bobsled

462. Battle of the Brothers

463. Brooks Robinson

464. Bucks

465. Houston Comets

466. British Open

467. Blue Jays

468. Bill Mueller

469. Liberty

470. Kansas City Royals

Questions 471-480

471. What number did Mickey Mantle wear before he was sent down to the minors in 1951?

472. What is the name of the trimmed tree trunk tossed in competition every year during the Highland Games in Scotland?

473. In 1985, the 49ers traded up to the Patriots 16th pick to acquire this wide receiver from Mississippi Valley State University. Not a bad move, he went on to score 208 TDs.

474. What running back became Super Bowl MVP for the Redskins after capturing their first NFL Title since 1942?

475. He won The Masters six times between 1963-1986. Name this golfing legend who was 46 years old when he won his final green jacket.

476. What baseball team played its only season at Sick's Stadium in 1969 before becoming the Milwaukee Brewers?

477. How many gold medals did Jesse Owens win at the 1936 Berlin Olympics?

478. In what country did the Mohammad Ali's "Rumble in the Jungle" take place?

479. The Kansas City Wizards won their first MLS Cup Championship in 2000, proving that the best defense could beat whose best offense in the league?

480. What did Jose Canseco hit in his very first career at-bat in the World Series?

Answers 471-480

471. 6

472. Caber

473. Jerry Rice

474. John Riggins

475. Jack Nicklaus

476. Seattle Pilots

477. 4

478. Zaire

479. Chicago Fire

480. Grand Slam

Questions 481-490

481. The North American Soccer League (NASL) existed from 1968-1984. The team from Ft. Lauderdale was called?

482. What sport did Anders Haugen receive a bronze medal for 50 years after he competed in 1924 Winter Olympics when a scoring error was discovered in 1974?

483. The scandal involving the New England Patriots' videotaping of the New York Jets defensive signals during a 2007 NFL game became known as what "-gate?"

484. What city in Arkansas hosts the Oak Lawn horse-racing track?

485. What's the name of Kansas City's MLB team? It may have been intended as a respectful nod to the Kansas City Monarchs, a Negro League team from 1920-1930.

486. What NBA player made 15,837 field goals during his career?

487. What NBA great is Ferdinand Lewis Alcindor, Jr. better known as?

488. The North American Soccer League (NASL) existed from 1968-1984. The team from Tampa Bay was called?

489. There are two MLB teams in Texas, the Houston Astros and this team that plays in Arlington.

490. This NBA team originated in Charlotte in 1998 and played there until 2002 when it moved to New Orleans, but for a brief two seasons played in Oklahoma City due to damage inflicted by Hurricane Katrina.

Answers 481-490

481. Strikers

482. Ski Jumping

483. Spygate

484. Hot Springs

485. Royals

486. Kareem Abdul-Jabbar

487. Kareem Abdul-Jabbar

488. Rowdies

489. Rangers

490. Hornets

Questions 491-500

491. What was Willie Mays' nickname?

492. What legendary football coach played for the New York Yankees 1919?

493. In their first season as a professional team in 1962, they posted a record of 40â€"120, also known as one of the worst regular season records since the MLB went to a 162-game season.

494. A pseudonym used by Washington Irving in his "A History of New York" referring to Dutch colonials of New York City influenced the name of this NBA team from New York City.

495. What NFL team has a pack of rabid fans known as the Dawg Pound?

496. What professional sport do the Baltimore Blast, Milwaukee Wave and Philadelphia KiXX compete in?

497. Which city hosted the Super Bowl three times out of the first five?

498. What was the original name of the Pittsburgh Steelers when they were founded in 1933?

499. In what country were the 1940 Sapporo Winter Olympic games cancelled?

500. Prior to getting this NHL team in 1998, various teams played for the city of Nashville in different leagues holding several names, including the Dixie Flyers, Ice Flyers, Knights, Nighthawks, Sounds and South Stars.

Answers 491-500

491. The Say Hey Kid

492. George Halas

493. New York Mets

494. Knicks

495. Browns

496. Indoor Soccer

497. Miami

498. Pirates

499. Japan

500. Predators

Questions 501-510

501. Which boxer was the first in history to become a septuple champion--holding seven world titles in seven different weight classes?

502. What expansion team joined the National League along with the Montreal Expos in 1969?

503. What type of car was the first to win the Indianapolis 500 in 1911?

504. How many points must a player win by in table tennis?

505. What NASL team boasted on its roster arguably the best offensive player, Pele, and the best defense player, Beckenbauer, of their time?

506. What Super Bowl was hosted on January 9, the earliest date in Super Bowl history? The Raiders defeated the Vikings by the score of 32â€"14.

507. What NFL team merged with the Philadelphia Eagles during WWII because the two teams had lost too many players to military service?

508. What women's professional sport features the teams Boston Breakers, Philadelphia Independence & Washington Freedom?

509. In what country were the first Winter Olympic Games held?

510. In 2003, he became the first Canadian to win a major championship. Name this lefty who won The Masters in 2003.

Answers 501-510

501. Manny Pacquiao

502. San Diego Padres

503. Marmon Wasp

504. 2

505. New York Cosmos

506. Super Bowl XI

507. Pittsburgh Steelers

508. Soccer

509. France

510. Mike Weir

Questions 511-520

511. What hockey player is nicknamed "The Great One?"

512. Who was "Ring Magazine's" first Fighter of the Year in 1928?

513. What team did special teamer Desmond Howard play for when he was chosen as the MVP in Super Bowl XXXI?

514. U.S. sprinter Wilma Rudolph won three gold medals at the 1960 Olympic Summer Games that were hosted in what city?

515. The North American Soccer League (NASL) existed from 1968-1984. The team from St. Louis was called?

516. Who was the first in NBA history to win five consecutive rebounding titles?

517. At the 2004 Athens Summer Olympics, the U.S. lost its first ever men's basketball game to this country.

518. While reading the newspaper at the kitchen table in "A Christmas Story," Mr. Parker angrily mentions the White Sox trading long-time pitcher Bill Dietrich, whose nickname was what?

519. What Canadian-born sports coach and inventor created the sport of basketball, and is often credited with introducing the first football helmet?

520. What Anaheim Angel won the 2003 MLB Home Run Derby?

Answers 511-520

511. Wayne Gretzky

512. Gene Tunney

513. Packers

514. Rome

515. Stars

516. Moses Malone

517. Puerto Rico

518. Bullfrog

519. James Naismith

520. Garret Anderson

Questions 521-530

521. Who was the head coach of the Kansas City Chiefs when they upset the undefeated Green Bay Packers in the 2011 regular season?

522. He's won league MVP honors in both the National and American Leagues. Name this player who won the triple crown in 1966 while playing for the Orioles.

523. Often called "The Hammer," what baseball legend broke Babe Ruth's home run record of 714 career runs on April 8, 1974?

524. The North American Soccer League (NASL) existed from 1968-1984. The team from New York was called?

525. It's the name for a college football rivalry game played by the Oregon Ducks and the Oregon State Beavers.

526. What type of sport suspends a person from a parachute dragged by a boat?

527. This was the name of the real boxer known as the "Cinderella Man" who delivered what many consider to be the greatest upsets in boxing history when he defeated Max Baer in a 1935 title bout.

528. Ninotchka, The Farmer's Daughter, Tina Ferrari and Debbie Debutant were just some of the combatants of the Gorgeous Ladies of Wrestling, known by what acronym?

529. Under the Marquess of Queensberry Rules, boxing matches became 3 minutes long, started using fair-sized gloves and officially reduced the count for fighter being knocked down to this many seconds.

530. What year saw the winner of The Masters receive the first Green Jacket?

Answers 521-530

521. Romeo Crennel

522. Frank Robinson

523. Hank Aaron

524. Cosmos

525. Civil War

526. Parasailing

527. James J. Braddock

528. GLOW

529. 10

530. 1949

Questions 531-540

531. Who was the first player on a losing team to be named Super Bowl MVP?

532. In what country was James Naismith--the inventor of basketbball--born?

533. During batting practice he collided head-first with Montreal Expos outfielder Tim Raines, who exclaimed, "You're a big unit!" Ever since, this 6'-10" fireballer has been known as the "Big Unit."

534. They were the Boston Patriots from inception until renamed the New England Patriots in 1971. However, what name was submitted & rejected by the NFL in 1971?

535. On June 15, 1972, several Seattle business and community leaders announced their intention to acquire an NFL franchise for the city. In 1975, the community named their team this synonym for an osprey.

536. Who was the first U.S. athlete to win a medal in both the Summer and Winter Olympics?

537. In ice hockey, if a player shoots the puck across at least two red lines, the last line being the opposing team's goal line, and the puck remains untouched by the passing team, what infraction took place?

538. The rivalry between the New York Giants and Dallas Cowboys, which started in 1960 with a 31-31 tie, was partly fueled by this fedora-wearing head coach who was the Giants defensive coordinator before joining Dallas.

539. In what country was volleyball invented?

540. What state does the Columbus Crew play its home games in?

Answers 531-540

531. Chuck Howley

532. Canada

533. Randy Johnson

534. Bay State Patriots

535. Seahawks

536. Eddie Eagan

537. Icing

538. Tom Landry

539. United States

540. Ohio

Questions 541-550

541. This Minnesota Twin won the American League's Rookie of the Year in 1967.

542. Who was the third person in the broadcast booth with Howard Cosell and Don Meredith when "Monday Night Football" debuted in 1970?

543. What Green Bay Packer became the first in Packers' history to throw 6 touchdowns in a game?

544. Who retired from the Chicago Bulls in 1993 and 1999?

545. What golfer went on to victory after being the ninth and final alternate for the PGA championship in 1991?

546. The 1934 St. Louis Cardinals MLB team were called what nickname?

547. What NBA player attempted 28,370 shots during his career?

548. What NBA athlete signed a 10-year endorsement deal with Gatorade in the early 90s, then claimed that Citrus Cooler was his favorite flavor?

549. What year were the first summer Olympic Games televised in the United States?

550. It's the official collegiate sports rivalry between the Baylor Bears and Texas A&M Aggies.

Answers 541-550

541. Rod Carew

542. Keith Jackson

543. Matt Flynn

544. Michael Jordan

545. John Daly

546. Gashouse Gang

547. Kareem Abdul-Jabbar

548. Michael Jordan

549. 1960

550. Battle of the Brazos

Questions 551-560

551. What sport was originally known as Mintonette?

552. How many points does a judge give the round winner in a boxing match?

553. In 1994, Columbus (Ohio) discovered this charter Major League Soccer team, though I doubt they ever sailed the ocean blue.

554. Tamika Catchings, Katie Douglas, and Australian Tully Bevilaqua have played for this WNBA team that's based in Indianapolis, Indiana.

555. Added to the MLB as an expansion franchise in 1977, this team was initially owned by the Labatt Brewing Company.

556. Who was first non-American to win the Masters when he became champion in 1961?

557. Who set a record for blocking 11 shots in one game during the 1989 NCAA basketball tournament?

558. Jersey Joe Walcott was the oldest heavyweight champion in history until he was ousted in 1994, when this boxer defeated Michael Moorer at the age of 45.

559. What 1932 Olympic runner was thought to be the first woman to break the 12-second barrier in the 100-meter race but was discovered to be a man after an autopsy in 1980?

560. What Heavyweight World Champion boxer retired an undefeated 49-0 in 1956?

Answers 551-560

551. Volleyball

552. 10

553. Crew

554. Fever

555. Toronto Blue Jays

556. Gary Player

557. Shaquille O'Neil

558. George Foreman

559. Stella Walsh

560. Rocky Marciano

Questions 561-570

561. This NBA basketball center played his entire career for the San Antonio Spurs. Due to his service as an officer in the United States Navy, he was nicknamed "The Admiral."

562. This NFL team was originally from Portsmouth, Ohio, and called the Portsmouth Spartans. It moved to Detroit in 1934 and changed its name to this animal, which the owner called the "monarch of the jungle."

563. The Atlas missile was developed in San Diego, which was home to this NBA team until they moved to Houston, in 1971.

564. This famous Kansas Citian was a baseball manager best known for guiding the Kansas City Royals to the World Series title in 1985.

565. What sporting event's official Latin motto means, "faster, higher, stronger?"

566. The official Olympic Flag was created by this French historian and founder of the modern Olympic Games.

567. Who made Green Bay Packer history when he jumped into the stands for the first ever Lambeau Leap on December 26, 1993?

568. In a 1997 fight, which would be extremely infamous and a dark day for boxing, Mike Tyson bit off a portion of what boxer's ear?

569. It's a college football rivalry game played by the Michigan Wolverines and the Ohio State Buckeyes.

570. What month is golf's Masters normally played?

Answers 561-570

561. David Robinson

562. Lions

563. Rockets

564. Dick Howser

565. Olympics

566. Pierre de Coubertin

567. Leroy Butler

568. Evander Holyfield

569. The Game

570. April

Questions 571-580

571. Los Angeles is home to the NBA's Lakers. However, there's another NBA team in L.A. What team is it?

572. This famous Kansas Citian was a baseball player whose pitching in the Negro leagues and in Major League Baseball made him a legend in his own lifetime.

573. What ABA player led the league with 803 steals in his career?

574. What two quarterbacks broke Dan Marino's 1984 single season passing yard record of 5,084 yards in 2011?

575. In Super Bowl XXXV on January 28, 2001, which NFL team did the Baltimore Ravens defeat, 34-7?

576. Who did Muhammad Ali defeat using the rope-a-dope strategy in the bout titled, "The Rumble in the Jungle?"

577. How many downs does a football team have to make another first down?

578. This charter ABA team was awarded to Kansas City, but moved to Denver in 1967 as the Larks, quickly changed its name to the Rockets and then to this NBA team name in 1974.

579. What is the term for two under par for a hole in golf?

580. Joe Namath played the most successful years of his career with this professional football team that has its stadium in one state and its name from another.

Answers 571-580

571. Clippers

572. Satchel Paige

573. Fatty Taylor

574. Drew Brees & Tom Brady

575. New York Giants

576. George Foreman

577. 4

578. Nuggets

579. Eagle

580. Jets

Questions 581-590

581. In 1981, what Montreal Expos player hit two home runs in the All-Star game?

582. Along with the Jacksonville Jaguars, this North Carolina team joined the NFL in 1995 as an expansion team. They appeared in Super Bowl XXXVIII, but lost 32-29 to the Patriots.

583. Who beat Jack Nicklaus and Johnny Miller for his last PGA tour win at the Bob Hope Desert Classic in 1973?

584. The New York Giants have a strange rivalry with this NFL team. It's strange because they both play their home games in the same stadium.

585. What college team did Magic Johnson's Michigan State team beat to become NCAA Champions in 1979?

586. Former Kansas football coach Don Fambrough exclaimed, "I'll die first!" when he referred to visiting a physician across what state line for treatment?

587. Edgar Allan Poe is buried in Baltimore, so the city paid homage to him by naming their NFL team what?

588. What state does Chivas USA play its home games in?

589. In what year did Michael Jordan win his last MVP award?

590. Freezing rain the night before the 1934 NFL Championship game prompted Ray Flaherty to remark that different shoes would provide better footing. Hence the game is now known by what name?

Answers 581-590

581. Gary Carter

582. Panthers

583. Arnold Palmer

584. NY Jets

585. Indiana State

586. Kansas-Missouri

587. Ravens

588. California

589. 1998

590. Sneakers Game

Questions 591-600

591. Whose ear did Mike Tyson find irresistibly tasty in a 1997 fight?

592. "Neon" Deion Sanders won the NFL Defensive Player of the Year award in 1995 with the San Francisco 49ers. What was his other nickname?

593. What women's basketball team became the first team in NCAA history to win 40 games in a season?

594. During the 20th century, only two countries won medals at every Summer Olympics. One was England, name the other country.

595. What college basketball great averaged more than 44 points a game and scored 3,667 points during his 3 seasons at LSU?

596. Who was the first player drafted by an NFL team to actually play an NFL game?

597. It's the name of an intense rivalry between athletic teams, with origins from the Civil War, from the University of Missouri Tigers and University of Kansas Jayhawks.

598. What is the corner doctor who's responsible for keeping a boxer's face and eyes free of cuts more commonly called?

599. What sport involves rolling down an incline in an inflatable sphere?

600. This Major League Baseball team originated in Brooklyn, New York, but moved to Los Angeles before the 1958 season.

Answers 591-600

591. Evander Holyfield

592. Prime Time

593. Baylor

594. France

595. Pistol Pete Maravich

596. Riley Smith

597. Border War

598. Cutman

599. Zorbing

600. Dodgers

Questions 601-610

601. Whose spectacular fourth quarter, 38-yard sideline catch did Bill Belichick challenge in the 2012 Super Bowl?

602. Against the Browns in 2003, what Ravens RB broke the NFL record for rushing yards in a game with 295 yards?

603. Who was the first player to win over $1,000,000 for winning the Masters Tournament?

604. This famous Arkansan was a professional baseball player best known as the first to break Ty Cobb's all-time major league stolen base record.

605. What Dodger pitcher allowed the St. Louis Cardinals' Fernando Tatis to hit two grand slams off him in the same inning on April 23, 1999?

606. In the third inning of an MLB game on April 23, 1999, this Cardinals player hit two grand slams off of Dodger pitcher Chan Ho Park... in the same inning!

607. It's the athletics rivalry between the University of Oklahoma Sooners and the Oklahoma State University Cowboys.

608. In what city did the Harlem Globetrotters make their first appearance after four decades of playing basketball?

609. At the 1900 Paris Olympics, Australian Frederick Lane won the gold medal in this unusual event.

610. This famous wild-haired flamboyant boxing promoter was responsible for the "Rumble in the Jungle" and the "Thrilla in Manila."

Answers 601-610

601. Mario Manningham

602. Jamal Lewis

603. Tiger Woods

604. Lou Brock

605. Chan Ho Park

606. Fernando Tatis

607. Bedlam Series

608. Harlem

609. Obstacle Race-Swimming

610. Don King

Questions 611-620

611. What city will host the 2016 Summer Olympics?

612. He was the founder or co-founder of the AFL, KC Chiefs, Chicago Bulls, KC Wiz, United Soccer Association and the MLS. His money came from oil, not ketchup.

613. This NBA team located in Philadelphia, PA, is named for the year America signed the Declaration of Independence.

614. What pro player's hitting streak ended after 56 straight games with a hit?

615. During the 2002 Winter Olympic Games, Russians Yelena Berezhnaya and Anton Sikharulidze were awarded gold medals despite a minor (but obvious) technical error in the former's routine which became known as what "-gate?"

616. Who won hockey's Art Ross Memorial Trophy a record ten times?

617. Name the athletic event where the object to be thrown is a heavy steel ball attached to a wire rope with a handle on the other end.

618. His nickname didn't include the bacon, but three Defensive Player of the Year awards and the MVP of the 1986 season definitely brought it home for this New York Giants great.

619. A new rule was added to NCAA football in 2010 that banned messages on eye paint, which this player frequently did by painting bible verses, like John 3:16, on his face.

620. From 1936 until 2000, only three men's teams have won Olympic basketball gold. Besides the U.S. and Russia, what is the other country?

Answers 611-620

611. Rio de Janeiro

612. Lamar Hunt

613. 76ers

614. Joe DiMaggio

615. Skategate

616. Wayne Gretzky

617. Hammer Throw

618. Lawrence "L.T." Taylor

619. Tim Tebow

620. Yugoslavia

Questions 621-627

621. In what city did the first Olympic torch relay end after 3,330 runners carried it through Greece, Bulgaria, Yugoslavia, Hungary, Austria, Czechoslovakia, and Germany?

622. Besides their notable achievement of being on the 2008 Olympic rowing team, twins Tyler and Cameron Winklevoss became multi-millionaires after a court battle with what website that they claimed stole their idea?

623. In what year did the Olympic rings officially debut?

624. What is the main association of men's national football (soccer) teams in North America, Central America and the Caribbean called?

625. For what sport do players often use speed glue on their rackets?

626. Named for the cities of St. Paul and Minneapolis, what's the name Minnesota's MLB team?

627. What DiMaggio led the league in runs in 1950 and 1951?

Answers 621-627

621. Berlin

622. Facebook

623. 1920

624. CONCACAF

625. Table Tennis

626. Twins

627. Dom DiMaggio. Nicknamed "The Little Professor", Dom DiMaggio was the younger brother of Vince and Joe Dimaggio.

.

ABOUT THE AUTHOR

Dr. Seven Phoenix (Doc) has hosted several popular pub trivia nights in Eugene, Oregon since early 2008. Seven Phoenix grew up in Pennsylvania, before moving to the Pacific Northwest, where he earned his Ph.D. in Sociology. Doc loves spending time with his English Mastiff, Kinsey, and enjoys hiking and exploring the Pacific Northwest (in the three months of the year when it isn't raining). You can email Doc at: Se7enPhoenix@gmail.com or follow him on twitter @Se7enPhoenix.

Made in the USA
Middletown, DE
21 July 2016